# moshi monsters™

# Super Moshi Missions

# SUNBIRD

Published by Ladybird Books Ltd 2012
A Penguin Company
Penguin Books Ltd, 80 Strand, London, WC2R 0RL, UK
Penguin Group (USA) Inc., 375 Hudson Street, New York 10014, USA
Penguin Books Australia Ltd, Camberwell Road, Camberwell, Victoria 3124,
Australia (A division of Pearson Australia Group Pty Ltd)
Penguin Group (NZ), 67 Apollo Drive, Rosedale, Auckland 0632,
New Zealand (a division of Pearson New Zealand Ltd)
Canada, India, South Africa

Sunbird is a trademark of Ladybird Books Ltd

Written by Steve Cleverley and Richard Dinnick
Illustrations by Vincent Bechet, Ross McCaughey and Trevor White

© Mind Candy Ltd. Moshi Monsters is a trademark
of Mind Candy Ltd. All rights reserved.

www.ladybird.com

ISBN: 978-1-40939 - 0930
001 - 10 9 8 7 6 5 4 3 2 1
Printed in Slovakia

# moshi monsters™

# Super Moshi Missions

# Contents

# Welcome, Super Moshis!

If it's guidance you seek, look no further, because I'm the all-seeing, **all-knowing leader** of the Super Moshis (as long as I'm wearing my contact lenses).

Better still, I know everything there is to know about . . . well, everything. How? Well some say I tumbled into the **mythical Well of Wisdom** when I was a baby and emerged chanting 'Ohmmmmm!' through my flowing beard. But that can't be true because I didn't have a beard in those days!

Needless to say I wasn't always known as Elder Furi. Once upon a time my monstery friends knew me as – yep, you guessed it – **Younger Furi.** But that was back when I was studying Superness at the **Super Moshiversity.** My real name is . . . no, I'm afraid my lips are sealed. Besides, it's **too risky.**

If you really want to know my name you'll have

to ask my old room-mate, **Lavender Troggs.** But that might prove difficult as he's . . . erm, let's just say he's rather difficult to contact these days.

Anyway, enough about me. Let's talk about recent events. Unless you've been living in the Twinkly Dink Mines you'll know that there's been a **whole heap of action** going on in the world of Moshi.

It was so serious I had to leave my remote hut in the foothills of Mount Sillimanjaro and re-open the abandoned **Super Moshi volcano HQ.** I was even forced to enlist a new troupe of Super Moshis to help me defeat Dr. Strangeglove and his evil C.L.O.N.C. colleagues. It was a **rip-roaring adventure** and my brave Super Moshis fought off goo, Glumps and glove-wearing villains – and those were just the things beginning with 'g'.

So iron your cape, slip on your mask and read all about it. This is going to be Super!

# History of the Super Moshis

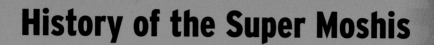

Yay! The Super Moshis are here to bring **peace, justice and the Moshi Way** to Monstro City. But this isn't the first time Super Moshis have saved the day. Their **heroic deeds** have been mentioned in many Moshistory books.

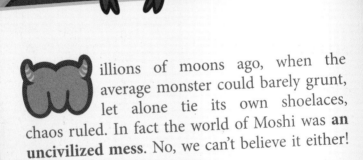

illions of moons ago, when the average monster could barely grunt, let alone tie its own shoelaces, chaos ruled. In fact the world of Moshi was **an uncivilized mess**. No, we can't believe it either!

But then one day, Moshi miners digging for umba thlunks (don't ask!) discovered an enormous **underground cavern.** Inside they found a huge clump of glowing rock – and it was shaking, juddering and quaking.

Not knowing any better, the miners shattered the wobbly rock. Inside they found a whole bunch of **sleeping Super Moshis.**

Before long the Super Moshis stirred from their slumber, slammed their fists against their chests,

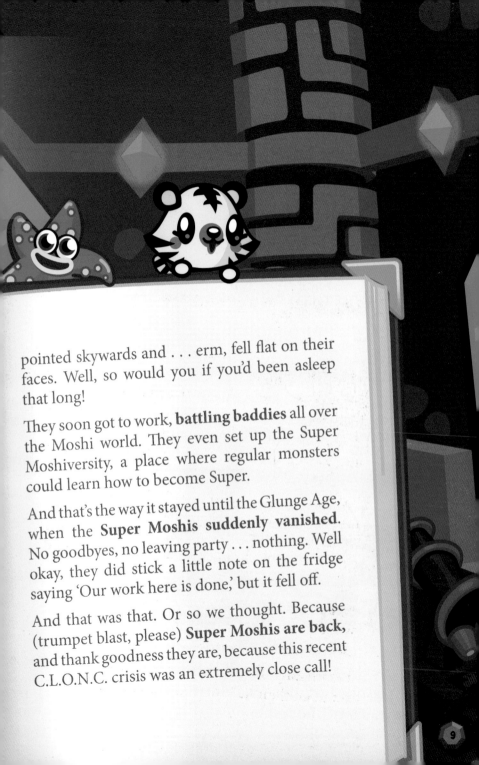

pointed skywards and . . . erm, fell flat on their faces. Well, so would you if you'd been asleep that long!

They soon got to work, **battling baddies** all over the Moshi world. They even set up the Super Moshiversity, a place where regular monsters could learn how to become Super.

And that's the way it stayed until the Glunge Age, when the **Super Moshis suddenly vanished**. No goodbyes, no leaving party . . . nothing. Well okay, they did stick a little note on the fridge saying 'Our work here is done,' but it fell off.

And that was that. Or so we thought. Because (trumpet blast, please) **Super Moshis are back,** and thank goodness they are, because this recent C.L.O.N.C. crisis was an extremely close call!

**Main Video Screen:** Great for watching MonstroVision, Moshi TV and the video to the Super Moshi March, this is the main screen for the volcano's Super Computer. (Also hides a nasty stain on the wall.)

**Flushing Chain:** Every now and then Elder Furi gives this an almighty pull in order to flush the volcano. Don't ask why, just marvel at the technology. Whoosh!!

**High-Powered MoshiScope:** Used to see what's going on in the outside world. Also good for shoo-ing Pilfering Toucans off the rim of the volcano.

**Elevator Plinth:** This stone platform opens up (as long as you have keys and Elder Furi's Magic Staff), giving access to the basement of the volcano.

# The Secret Volcano HQ

What exactly lies within this mysterious, super cool base? Check out this highly informative diagram (but don't show it to anyone, it's supposed to be secret).

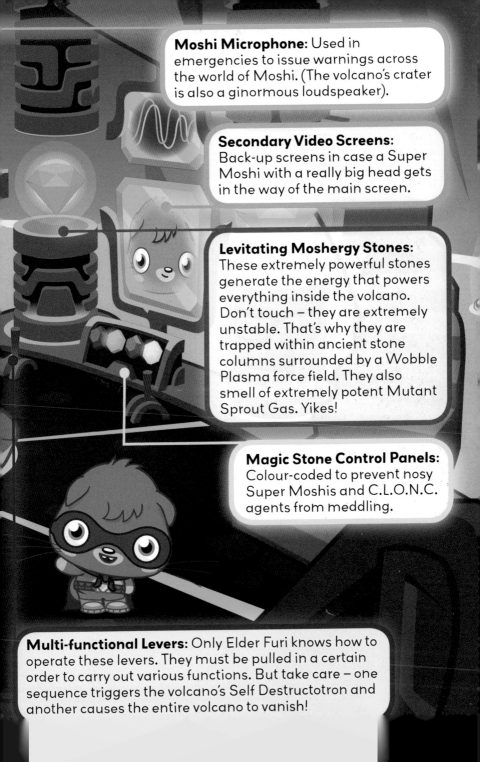

**Moshi Microphone:** Used in emergencies to issue warnings across the world of Moshi. (The volcano's crater is also a ginormous loudspeaker).

**Secondary Video Screens:** Back-up screens in case a Super Moshi with a really big head gets in the way of the main screen.

**Levitating Moshergy Stones:** These extremely powerful stones generate the energy that powers everything inside the volcano. Don't touch – they are extremely unstable. That's why they are trapped within ancient stone columns surrounded by a Wobble Plasma force field. They also smell of extremely potent Mutant Sprout Gas. Yikes!

**Magic Stone Control Panels:** Colour-coded to prevent nosy Super Moshis and C.L.O.N.C. agents from meddling.

**Multi-functional Levers:** Only Elder Furi knows how to operate these levers. They must be pulled in a certain order to carry out various functions. But take care – one sequence triggers the volcano's Self Destructotron and another causes the entire volcano to vanish!

# Super Moshi Manifesto

Super Moshis are dedicated to **battling baddies**, vanquishing fear and **blasting C.L.O.N.C.** to the Way-Outta-Sphere. But it's not just about defeating naughty critters. Super Moshis fight for peace, justice and the Moshi Way!

Check out the Super Moshi Manifesto to see if you've got what it takes to kick C.L.O.N.C. out of Monstro City (All Super Moshis must learn this by heart).

# Super Moshi Manifesto

- Always make sure your cape is ironed. A neat Super Moshi is a happy Super Moshi.

- Never remove your mask. Revealing your true identity could have disastrous consequences.

- Respect your elders, especially Furi ones.

- Always wipe your feet before entering the Super Moshi volcano HQ.

- Always help old monsters to cross Main Street, even if you're on an urgent mission.

- Never accept sweets from Sweet Tooth (they are probably rotten).

- Do not dance to that terrible song by Dr. Strangeglove.

- Do not mix with known C.L.O.N.C. associates.

- Always raise your hands and stomp your feet when you hear the Super Moshi March.

- Always wear your pants OVER your tights. (Just joking).

- Keep your Magic Stones (Morph Stone, etc.) safe and sound.

- Recite the words to the Super Moshi March every morning.

# What Does it Take to Become a Super Moshi?

In order to become a Super Moshi it's essential to learn the Super Moshi Manifesto and the Super Moshi March **off by heart.** You must also iron your cape every day and practise putting your eye-mask on **with your feet** (you never know when your hands might be tied up by Dr. Strangeglove). Always be ready to **drop everything** (even your ice scream) when Elder Furi or the Gatekeeper summons you to Super Moshi HQ.

**Regular exercise is vital.** We're not just talking about putting your hands on your hips and raising both fists in the air, superhero-style. We're talking about star jumps, somersaults and that tricksy thing where you **pat your head and rub your tummy** at the same time.

But being Super is not all about working up a sweat. You'll need to **give your brain a daily workout** too.

Try to unscramble one egg and untangle at least two pretzels every morning. You can also do a bit of algebra as you attempt to put your toothpaste back in the tube. Working out the square root of a banana whilst counting to a squillion is also **highly beneficial.**

As you can tell, being a Super Moshi is **monsterrifically hard work** and you'll need to **stay on your toes** – rumour has it Elder Furi can make you un-Super with just a wave of his Magic Staff. **So what are you waiting for?** 'Hup, two, three, four . . .'

# C.L.O.N.C.

C.L.O.N.C. (short for **'Criminal League of Naughty Critters'**) is the mysterious organisation that has brought mischief and mayhem to Monstro City and beyond. But what is **C.L.O.N.C.'s masterplan?** And who is behind this rascally band of villains? Here's what we know...

There were rumours of C.L.O.N.C.'s existence long before Dr. Strangeglove appeared. In fact, Moshi criminologists believe that this **shadowy collection of baddies** have been **plotting to take over Monstro City** and beyond for ages. But who pays for all their awesome contraptions, super weapons, vehicles and Glumping machines? Word on the street (okay, it was Bubba the Bouncer) says that C.L.O.N.C. has **friends in high places** – rich friends to be precise. Any ideas who they could be?

Despite lots of investigation, no Moshi knows for sure how many naughty critters are involved with C.L.O.N.C. Obviously Dr. Strangelove and Sweet Tooth are high rankin employees, but spies have spotted at least **ten (!!) more crooks** sitting around the C.L.O.N.C. conference table.

**Mwaa-ha haa!**

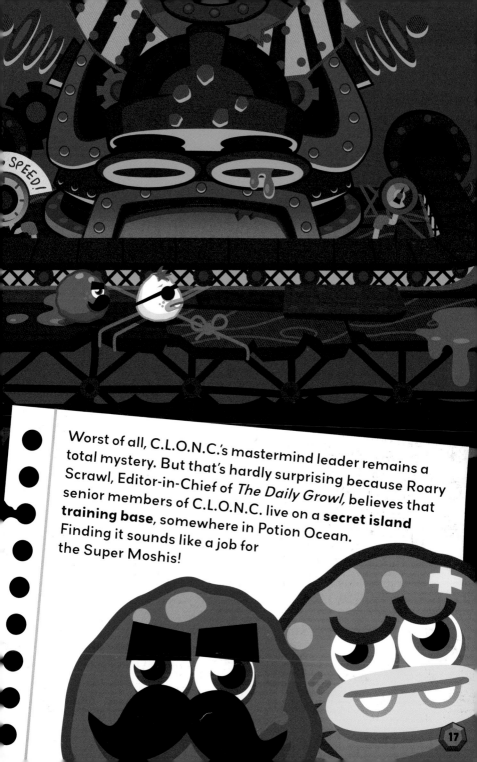

Worst of all, C.L.O.N.C.'s mastermind leader remains a total mystery. But that's hardly surprising because Roary Scrawl, Editor-in-Chief of *The Daily Growl,* believes that senior members of C.L.O.N.C. live on a **secret island training base**, somewhere in Potion Ocean. Finding it sounds like a job for the Super Moshis!

SPEED!

# MISSION 1:
## Missing Moshling Egg

Something terrible has happened at Buster Bumblechops' **Incubation Station!** Some vagabond has stolen a **rare Moshling Egg!** Look for clues and help the Moshling Expert find his **missing egg.**

## Part 1: The Incubation Station

Poor Buster Bumblechops! There's nothing he doesn't know about Moshlings. Except of course, what has happened to his latest Moshling egg!

### WHAT'S THE DEAL?
### BUSTER BUMBLECHOPS

Buster Bumblechops is Monstro City's top Moshling expert. He keeps all the teeny-weeny creatures at his secret ranch. He often appears in the *Daily Growl*, writing about exotic Moshlings and he's even written a book about them - *The Moshling Collector's Guide*. So if anyone can help you find out more about the missing Moshling egg, it's him!

You'll need to hunt high and low in the Incubation Station to find clues. This is a crime scene, right? So you'll have to play the detective. Did the thief leave any marks behind or break anything when they stole the Moshling egg? Get investigating!

When Buster has all the clues, you can start on the trail of the thief who took the egg!

# ELDER FURI'S TRAINING TIPS:

**Being a Super Moshi doesn't just mean wearing your pants outside your trousers! It also means using your head!**

- **If something you find doesn't work on one thing, try it on another!**
- **You might pick up stuff that will be useful later in the mission - not necessarily where you first discover it.**
- **Search carefully - clues might be hidden or even locked away!**

# Part 2: The Wobbly Woods

There are lots of amazing plants and critters in the Wobbly Woods. I often walk there myself, trying not to trip over my beard and pondering how we might defeat Dr. Strangeglove. And there's nothing better for a good ponder than staring at a lovely, clear pond!

While you're there, check out all the flowers and different coloured berries. Keep an eye out for all three types – yellow, red and blue. But don't scoff them all, you might need them for something else . . .

A Super Moshi should make friends with everyone they meet. You never know who might be able to help you on your quest.

## WHAT'S THE DEAL?
# SHREWMAN

He's very shy but he can be helpful. He loves writing stories on his tippy-tappy typewriter and he also loves berries. Some say he squishes them and uses them as ink! But he hardly ever leaves the safety of his tree trunk home so maybe you can tempt him to come out if you give him a treat?

## WHAT'S THE DEAL?
# PROFESSOR PURPLEX

Owls of Wiseness can often be found high in the trees of Wobbly Woods. But they don't like being disturbed while reading. Although if they finish a book, they are always looking for more reading/nibbling material! (Just make sure you're not wearing a bowler hat, though! They're not very fond of those.)

# ELDER FURI'S TRAINING TIPS:

You've got to have a bit of patience if you're going to be a Super Moshi!

- Monsters you meet might be too busy to talk to you, so let them get on with whatever they're doing and come back to them later. Then they might be ready to give you a hand!
- At first it might not be obvious how an item will come in useful, but don't worry, you'll soon get the hang of it.

## SUPER MOSHI MISSION HINT

Keep your super senses about you and **watch out** for **movement** or **sounds** that may be extra clues.

# Part 3: The Secret Hideout

Now, battling Dr. Strangeglove can get a bit creepy. Don't worry. Remember that he's so horrible even those who work for him can sometimes be persuaded to help you!

If you're going into Dr Strangeglove's secret hideout, you'll soon find out he's a terribly messy evil genius! He probably got into all sorts of trouble with mummy Strangeglove when he was little for not tidying his room.

But his untidiness is great for us! He's left lots of stuff everywhere, like bones, potion bottles, books, secret ingredients and – be prepared – some really yukky stuff, too!

# CODE RED HELP!

## The Hero's Reward:

## Lady Goo Goo

Some say she's crazy, some say she's a genius. One thing's for sure, the Moshi world has gone completely gooey for Lady Goo Goo the Glitzy Boo Hoo – and now you can too!

# MISSION 2:
## Voyage Under Potion Ocean

That super sneaky **Dr. Strangeglove** is stealing Fishies from the beach! Find Cap'n Buck aboard the *Cloudy Cloth Clipper* and together you can uncover **Strangeglove's evil plan.**

## Part 1: Bleurgh Beach

Bleurgh Beach is a sandy paradise where Moshlings of all kinds enjoy the sun, sea and sand. Gail Whale swims there and monsters often head there to soak up some rays. It's usually fun and friendly, but Fumble's been snatched from his sunbathing spot! Is no one safe from Strangeglove?

## WHAT'S THE DEAL?
# FUMBLE

These Acrobatic SeaStars live amongst the coral reefs of Bleurgh Lagoon but often gather on the beach. They are pretty fearless and love to perform death-defying stunts!

This is a water based mission – so you're going to need a boat and the bigger the better! Captain Buck has a big galleon but you'll need to get to him first.

# ELDER FURI'S TRAINING TIPS:

• Remember to keep your eyes at hand - go beachcombing and pick up everything you can find!

25

# Part 2: Aboard Captain Buck's Boat

Once you clamber aboard the *Cloudy Cloth Clipper*, you'll find Cap'n Buck E. Barnacle! He'll help any Super Moshi in trouble but first you've got to help him get his ship ready to sail!

## WHAT'S THE DEAL?
## CAP'N BUCK E. BARNACLE

Lost at sea when he was just a little Barnacle, Cap'n Buck was raised by a school of Batty Bubblefish. Buck began a life of piracy, captaining the *Cloudy Cloth Clipper* and finding booty all over the seventy seas. Rumour has it he keeps something precious in his treasure chest ...

Even when the ship's clean and ready to go, a Captain needs a compass and Buck is always leaving his lying around. Last time we found it at the Underground Disco – but then he never could find his way around the dance floor!

While you're tracking it down, Lefty will have been on the lookout in the crow's nest and he might have spotted some places for you to check out!

# ELDER FURI'S TRAINING TIPS:

**Life can be a bit of a puzzle, young Super Moshi!
But we laugh in the face of puzzles by training hard!**

- Watch out for unusual things, like unexpected goo.
- Leave no stone unturned, no island unvisited.
- Remember: a Super Moshi always has the right tools for the job!

## SUPER MOSHI MISSION HINT

Lefty might have spotted some strange goo on the horizon but you're the one who has to plot the course to get the ship there!

# Part 3: Under the Sea

Now you've got to find out what's at the bottom of the sea, causing all that goo to come to the surface! If you find Dr. Strangeglove's undersea lair – be careful! He's as dangerous as a snake with a headache!

That hatted hater of happiness has all sorts of nasty machines for turning Moshlings into Glumps. I wish we could smash them all! Perhaps you can break this one ... you never know what you might find inside!

## SUPER MOSHI MISSION HINT

If you're going underwater, use your awesome **sonar waves** to push over stuff that's in your way out. Be careful though, the sub is fitted with a shield but it won't last forever if you keep knocking into stuff.

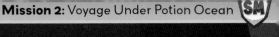

## CODE RED HELP!

## The Hero's Reward:

### Wurley

Thanks to their motor-rotary headgear these tin-skinned Moshlings can quickly transport Rox and other precious thingies across the world of Moshi. As they wokka-wokka their way through the clouds, tiddlycopters love humming classical music and performing loop-the-loops. Weeee!

# MISSION 3:
## Strangeglove from Above

This is an **AIR ALERT!** **Strangeglove** is **terrorising the Fluffies** in the clouds above Monstro City! **Super Moshis** must take to the sky to **stop him!**

## Part 1: Among the Clouds

Those poor Fluffies. We must save them! Quickly! To the Moshi-planes! We have a whole squadron so we should be able to make Strangeglove flee! But the evil genius is a fiend! He has a huge airship filled with hot air – probably from all the orders he gives to his Glumps! You'll need to call on lots of fluffy friends to help you find your way over the rainbow in this mission! (Keep an eye out for C.L.O.N.C. candies in the cloud city . . .)

## WHAT'S THE DEAL?
# NIMBUS

Nimbus is a cloud who lives the high life! But don't confuse her with Dipsy. With Dinky Dreamclouds, you've got to get 'em angry to make it rain. With Nimbus, it's jokes that open her taps! But when you upset her, things can get real stormy!

**C.L.O.N.C**

## WHAT'S THE DEAL?
# I.G.G.Y.

I.G.G.Y. is a pixel-munching Moshling who's unpredictable, hyper and bouncy! He loves to snaffle up your computer cursor the moment he sees it, but he can be handy for other stuff, too.

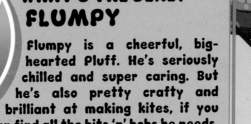

## WHAT'S THE DEAL?
# FLUMPY

Flumpy is a cheerful, big-hearted Pluff. He's seriously chilled and super caring. But he's also pretty crafty and brilliant at making kites, if you can find all the bits 'n' bobs he needs.

31

# Part 2: On Scare Force One

We've learnt the hard way that Strangeglove's airship has too many goo guns! We always get splattered no matter how many planes we send against it. What you need to do is get inside the airship somehow!

The cool thing about having Moshlings like Wurley along with you is that they can get into places you might not fit!

Everything aboard the airship is powered by stinky, yucky Goo! Most of the time, this will be inside pipes so you don't have to hold your nose too much. Poo-ee! If you can control the Goo, who knows what you can do?

## SUPER MOSHI MISSION HINT

Always keep your eyes peeled for **escape routes!**

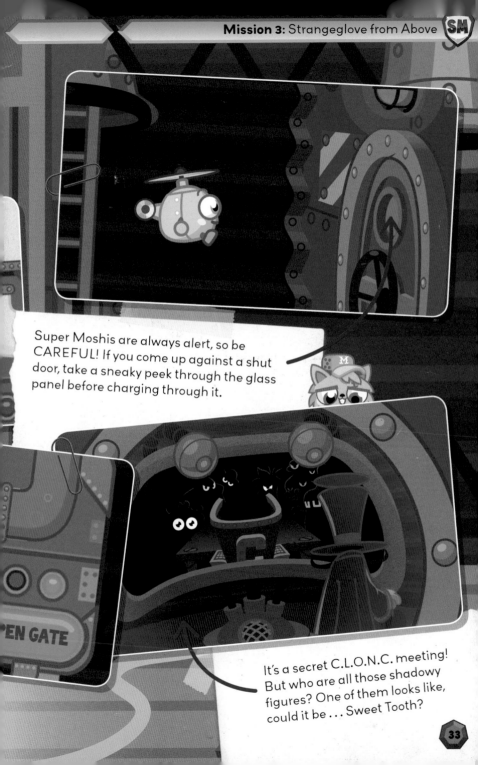

Super Moshis are always alert, so be CAREFUL! If you come up against a shut door, take a sneaky peek through the glass panel before charging through it.

It's a secret C.L.O.N.C. meeting! But who are all those shadowy figures? One of them looks like, could it be . . . Sweet Tooth?

**33**

GOO PRESSURE   GOO PRES.

## WHAT'S THE DEAL?
# SWEET TOOTH

Sweet Tooth is a sickly psycho and a leading member of C.L.O.N.C. This deliciously evil candy criminal never goes anywhere without a big bag of tooth-decaying treats and a Hypno Blaster lollipop. No one knows if Sweet Tooth is a he or a she. Just don't ask! The last monster that did ended up in moshpital, wearing a gobstopper!

# ELDER FURI'S TRAINING TIPS:

Always be on the look out for Strangeglove's weird machines and gadgets . . .

- If they're broken, see if you can fix them - they might be useful!
- Try and sabotage any dangerous-looking machinery. You should know by now that sticking a spanner in the works is a really good idea when it comes to Strangeglove!

# CODE RED HELP!

⊙◇ ℧Ξ⋈ Φ⊣⅃Ⴤ∃⊣∩⊡ ℧≺⅃◇
℧Ξ⋈ ∩⊣∩⊡⋈⅄ ⊙◇ ℔℧⅃Φ◇⁎⋈
⁎⋈⊙ⵙ⋈ ℔ ⅄Φ∇Ξ⊣◇⋈ ℧⊙
⊙∩⋈◇ ℧Ξ⋈ ▣⊙⊙⅃

## The Hero's Reward:

## Plinky

One of the ultra-rare Tunies, Plinky are squeezy-wheezy musical Moshlings. They loves having their keys tickled as they boing up and down, puffing out merry tunes and waltzing around town. But don't push their buttons - it makes 'em hiccup out of tune!

# MISSION 4:
## Candy Catastrope

Someone has been **selling dodgy candies** right under the nose of **Snozzle Wobbleson** from the Gross-ery Store! Help him find out who's behind **Dastardly Delights Candy** and stop the Monsters of Monstro City getting sick!

## Part 1: At the Gross-ery

For this one, you're gonna need to go deep, deep, deep undercover, Super Moshi! So you'll need a great disguise. I've got a Morph Stone that can make you look like a chump! Er. No, that's not right ... I mean it can make you look like a Glump! Yes. That's more like it. Now, to make the transformation, you'll need to find some smelly, sticky Glump Goo! But, first stop should be the Gross-ery.

You'll need to go behind the scenes and have a chat with Snozzle Wobbleson, the Gross-ery Store owner.

Give Snozzle a hand tidying up and you could find something that doesn't belong. Keep a note of any juicy information you discover – just DON'T EAT the evil candies.

## WHAT'S THE DEAL?
# SNOZZLE WOBBLESON

**Snozzle Wobbleson started out as a Gross-ery Stock Monster so he's very familiar with the storeroom! He was promoted to cashier after dropping sixteen cartons of eggs and making a real mess of things. Snozzle loves his job, especially creating new and tasty treats.**

## SUPER MOSHI MISSION HINT

All the candy in Monstro City comes from the **Candy Cane Caves**, so make that your next stop on the investigation.

# Part 2: The Candy Cane Caves

If C.L.O.N.C. are involved and there are evil sweets being sold at the Gross-ery, it's as certain as my beard is long that the Candy Cane Caves have been taken over by Dr. Strangeglove's mischievious sidekicks – the Glumps!

Be on the lookout for Green Glump Goo to use with the Morph Stone. Then you can disguise yourself as one of Strangeglove's crew.

There are Moshlings in the mines who might be able to help you, but now you've Glumped yourself, can you prove you're really a Super Moshi? Also in the mine you'll come across Roarkers. They would never normally work for that terrible Sweet Tooth so they must be under some kind of sweet spell . . .

## WHAT'S THE DEAL?
# ROARKERS

The Roarkers are the furry little construction workers of Monstro City. These ones happily dig and delve to produce the sweet delights in the Candy Cane Caves.

# ELDER FURI'S TRAINING TIPS:

- Glumps aren't too bright so you should be able to distract them somehow!

## SUPER MOSHI MISSION HINT

The trouble with the Morph Stone is that it will make you **look** like a Glump but it won't make you **smell** like one! You'll need to collect lots of stinky stuff so that you give off the right stench.

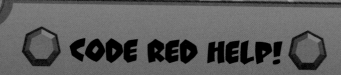

## CODE RED HELP!

▽⧫χ⌿⌿·⊡⊙⌿⊡ ×⧓ИИ ⧓⌇
⌒И⊙⊡× ⧓⧓ ⧫⧫ ✴×◊◊
⊡И◊◊⊙×⊡ ⊡·⧫ ◊◊·◊⧫◊⧫✴

### SUPER MOSHI MISSION HINT

Remember, Super Moshi, sometimes a Moshling's power can be useful even if it is dangerous. Learn to harness it against the villains you meet!

# Part 3: Sweet Tooth's Lair

Now you're on the fast track to Sweet Tooth's hideout!
Be very careful of Sweet Tooth – that sugary sweet face
hides a wicked mind and you don't want to end up on the
receiving end of that powerful Hypno-Blaster!

## The Hero's Reward:

### Cherry Bomb

This Baby Boomer has an explosive
personality, but don't panic, they
rarely go BOOM! Cherry Bombs
just love to fizzle with excitement,
but keep them away from water or
you'll dampen their spirits! Fzzzt!

# MISSION 5:
## Pop Goes the Goo Goo

Buster Bumblechops needs your help again! Lady Goo Goo has lost her voice! That Dr. Strangeglove – or one of his C.L.O.N.C. companions – has to be behind it! The Super Moshis must investigate!

## Part 1: The Incubation Station

Head back to Buster's Incubation Station again and ask the whiskered one some questions and you might start to get an idea of what's going on! When you're done there, your next stop will probably be Growl Mansion ...

As one of the biggest talents in all of Monstro City, Lady Goo Goo is bound to have attracted the attention of Simon Growl. I don't think he's working for Dr. Strangeglove. He's got too much talent for that but when it comes to stars, he really thinks he has the M factor!

"WALLOP"

SUSPECTED LOCATION
– THWACK BOOM VALLEY

# Part 2: Growl Mansion

## WHAT'S THE DEAL?
# SIMON GROWL

On the rare occurrence that Simon Growl doesn't tell you what he really thinks, you can always look at his hair to find out how he feels. Despite being voted meanest judge three years in a row, Simon is still the greatest (and only!) talent scout in Monstro City.

# ELDER FURI'S TRAINING TIPS:

Here are some top tips for dealing with Simon Growl:

- Remember that Simon is vain and always worried what he looks like. He always wants to know what other Monstro City celebs are up to.
- If you can use your loaf and come up with something cool to tell him, he might rush off to see what you're talking about ...
- He's nowhere near as good at looking after Moshlings as Buster is!

## SUPER MOSHI MISSION HINT

Sweep Lady Goo Goo's dressing room for things you can use to make a baby stop crying! (And I'm not talking about Simon Growl! I'm talking about Goo Goo!)

43

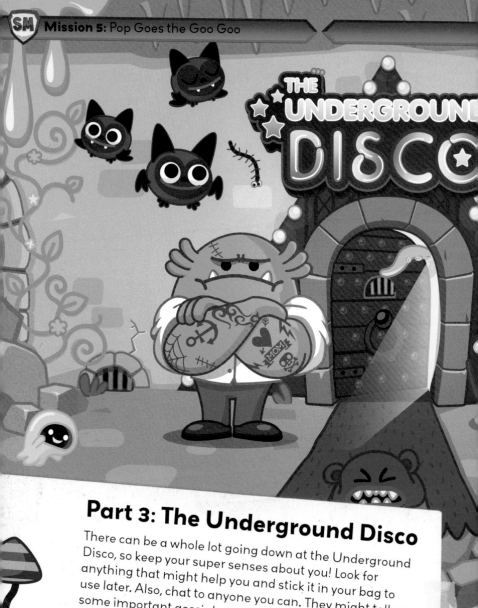

# Part 3: The Underground Disco

There can be a whole lot going down at the Underground Disco, so keep your super senses about you! Look for anything that might help you and stick it in your bag to use later. Also, chat to anyone you can. They might tell you some important gossip!

If you're headed to the Disco, you'll have to get past Bubba, the bouncer. He looks real tough – and he is – but if you can impress him he might let you into the Disco itself. And that could be really useful to your mission . . .

## WHAT'S THE DEAL?
# BUBBA

Bubba is a prominent tattoo artist and works at the Underground Disco as a bouncer. He loves practising his moves at home on his Dance, Dance, Roarvolution machine and hopes to show off his style in an upcoming dance-off!

## CODE RED HELP!

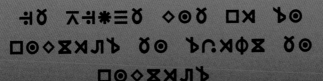

## WHAT'S THE DEAL?
# BONKERS

Possibly the only one of her kind, Bonkers has learned to do tricks to make enough Rox for her rent at Sludgetown Apartments. Bonkers' favourite food is Pop Rox.

# Part 4: The Musical Cave

You might have to ask for some help from your new friends to get into C.L.O.N.C.'s secret base nearby. I'll bet you need to have an ear for music too!

If you manage to get inside the evil lair, find out why they've taken Lady Goo Goo's voice. It's a really strong voice, perhaps they're using it as some kind of weapon? Watch out for the Robo-Quack C.L.O.N.C. agents and see if you can turn their tech against them!

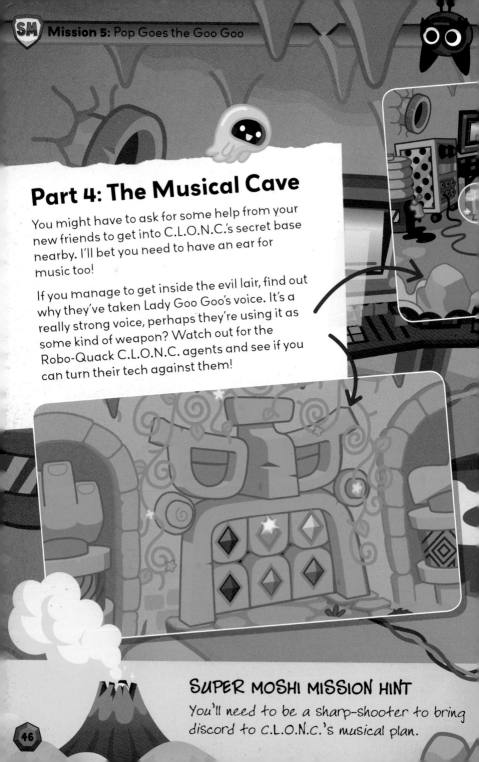

## SUPER MOSHI MISSION HINT

You'll need to be a sharp-shooter to bring discord to C.L.O.N.C.'s musical plan.

## WHAT'S THE DEAL?
# SPROCKETT & HUBBS

C.L.O.N.C. secret agent Sprockett ordered the Robo-Quacks to steal Lady Goo Goo's voice! Look out for him and his partner Hubbs in later missions!

## The Hero's Reward:

# Holga

Holga's a Happy Snappy and they just love to snap people's photos! If there's a famous monster in town, Holga is bound to be nearby!

47

# MISSION 6:
## Super Moshiversity Challenge

Dear Super Moshi, now that you've completed a few missions successfully, we think you're ready to attend the Super Moshiversity. Report to me immediately for a full briefing and don't forget to pack! Yours, Elder Furi.

## Part 1: In Your Room

So, you're off to Super Moshiversity? Hasn't the time flown? I remember when you were just starting out! Sniff. Well, I'm sure that you'll do very well.

The first thing you'll do at Moshiversity is meet your roomie. I think the headmaster said it would be Hermitty Ginger. She's a cool Super Moshi and I'm sure she'll help you settle in.

You've probably packed some stuff to take with you – I remember I did. I took pictures of my favourite Moshlings, my cuddly human, my stick (more of a twig back then) and a lot of shampoo for my beard. Once you have unpacked, take a good look around your new home.

Have you been studying your Super Moshi code? Keep an eye out for hidden messages in the Moshiversity! Strangeglove always loved to study his glyphs as a student, back in the day ...

## WHAT'S THE DEAL?
# THE HEADMASTER

Hmmm. We don't know very much about the Moshiversity's Headmaster, so see what you can discover. Could it be just a coincidence that he looks like Mustachio, one of Dr. Strangeglove's Glumps ...?

# Part 2: Class Time!

Now it's time to get down to some hard work. Make sure you aren't late for class! Hermitty will help you find it.

You'll be given textbooks to learn stuff from. Some of them will probably have the names of old students in them. You might even come across a book that used to belong to my old mate Hairy Rotter – he was always really good at spelling and wand-ering about the place!

Pay attention to everything you learn – there will probably be a test!

## SUPER MOSHI MISSION HINT

Make sure you've tidied all the shelves properly!

# ELDER FURI'S TRAINING TIPS:

**Memorise the powers of the Power Stones:**

- **Minime Stone** - used to transform Moshis into their baby selves
- **Morph Stone** - transforms Super Moshis into other monsters
- **Sonic Sapphire** - used to hypnotise and confuse!

# Part 3: Night Terrors

Your first night in your dorm room is a bit of a nightmare! Strange things are happening and someone has turned the room upside down! Use all your Super Moshi senses to work out what's going on and put things back in order.

# CODE RED HELP!

# Part 4: Missing Moshis!

Oh no! The headmaster is working for C.L.O.N.C.! While he is distracted, have a poke about in his lair to see if there's anything you can use to put a stop to his dastardly plan before it's too late!

## WHAT'S THE DEAL?
## MUSTACHIO

Is that facial fuzz for real or is it just a terrible disguise? Who knows because Mustachio is too busy barking orders and attacking Moshlings with scritchy-scratchy Bristly Brush Offs to answer silly questions.

## SUPER MOSHI MISSION HINT
Keep an eye out for clues about other C.L.O.N.C. activities while you're nosing about.

# The Hero's Reward:

## Penny

Penny is a Mini Money Moshling. They love flipping themselves high in the air, especially when they need to make an important decision! If you rub Penny on its tummy, it might just bring you good luck!

# MISSION 7:
## 20,000 Leagues Under the Fur

Something awful has happened at the Volcano! **Purple smoke is pouring out** across Monstro City! Head down there straight away and see what's going on . . .

## Part 1: The Empty Volcano Base

Elder Furi's gone missing! There's nobody to help the Super Moshis out on this task, we have to get Elder Furi back! You'll need to crack Elder Furi's password to hack into the computer system, but I'm sure a clever Super Moshi like you can do that. Right?

It's just as well you've graduated from Super Moshiversity because Elder Furi has protected his password with tricky questions – I hope you have been paying attention in class? Good luck!

Once you've accessed the computer, you might find that things have changed at HQ and you can use something you've picked up to help you solve this first mystery . . .

## WHAT'S THE DEAL?
## ELDER FURI

One of the wisest and most mysterious monsters in Monstro City, Elder Furi is the leader of the Super Moshis and old Moshiversity friend of Dr. Strangeglove!

## SUPER MOSHI MISSION HINT

Clicking on the padlock could give you the key!

55

# Part 2: Tamara's Secret Lab

Ah, right. You found me, then. Well done. Sorry about all the secrecy, but this is too serious to let everyone know what's happened!

Don't panic, but Elder Furi is very sick. He's got a bad case of the Glumps and I need you to go inside his body and cure him! But first you've gotta get inside my mini submarine so I can shrink it down.

To do that, we need some ingredients for a microscopic strength shrinking potion. Do you know where you can find some?

### Tamara Tesla's Make-All-Smallest Potion

Add the following to a cauldron:

1 x Tiki feather
1 x Minime stone
1 x lock of Elder Furi's hair
2 x drops troll snot
3 x batty bat droppings

# WHAT'S THE DEAL?
# TAMARA TESLA

Reared in a giant petri dish in Variable Valley, Tamara Tesla is Monstro City's own brainy scientist. She has a lab set up at the Observatory at The Port, where she invents new puzzles for The Puzzle Palace.

# WHAT'S THE DEAL?
# R.O.S.S

R.O.S.S stands for Robotic Operations Subdermal Submarine. A quick squirt of Tamara's potion will help him get you under the skin of any problem!

## SUPER MOSHI MISSION HINT
Give the bat a tickle!

# Part 3: Inside Elder Furi!

Now, it's time for you to go where no Super Moshi has ever gone before – inside Elder Furi! When you reach Elder Furi's brain, you'll find that the Glumps have messed up his memories. That's why he's so ill. You'll need to put his memories back in order and clean up those Glumps!

Keep your super senses about you as you trawl through his memories – Elder Furi could give you some clues about C.L.O.N.C.!

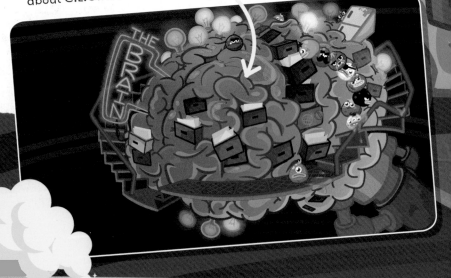

## SUPER MOSHI MISSION HINT
Use the toothbrush to scrub way the Glumps.

# CODE RED HELP!

ႦჄႸ ႶᲐ∇ᲧႦ⊲ႦჄᎭ Φ◇◪ ႦჄႸ
⧓ᲧႩ◇❋ ∇ΦჁ⧓◇ᏏႦჄ ΦႦჄ
∇⊙Ⴖ⊙⊲Ⴖ ∇⊙◪ჄᏏ

## The Hero's Reward:

# Tiamo

Tiamo is a Sparkly Sweetheart. These super rare Moshlings can appear out of nowhere to help monsters in distress. They also love a kicking beat!

# MISSION 8:
## Spooktacular Spectacular

You are cordially invited to Simon Growl's spooktacular Halloween party. It will be a great chance for you to chill out at the Haunted Mansion. If you dare . . .

## Part 1: Talk to the Hair Because the Face ain't There!

Ah, I see you've got an invite to the social event of the year! Simon Growl's parties are the best and most exclusive! I wish I could go, but all that dancing and jelly doesn't agree with me these days.

You go and have a great time. But remember, my young Super Moshi, always be alert for C.L.O.N.C. activities. With all the A-list celebs of Monstro City there, this is just the sort of party they'd love to crash!

If something does happen, it's likely it'll be Simon himself that C.L.O.N.C. are targeting. He is the most famous talent show judge in Monstro City, after all.

Keep your eyes peeled for any hair-raising happenings and things that go bump in the night!

# WHAT'S THE DEAL?
# SIMON GROWL'S HAIR

Not much is known about Simon Growl's hair, but he's never far away from the great monster himself. He must know all Simon's secrets . . .

# ELDER FURI'S TRAINING TIPS:

- Mingle with all the guests
- The mansion is haunted, but don't be afraid to explore - not all ghosts are scary!

61

# Part 2: The Eyes Have It!

Missing mogul mystery! Simon has vanished! You'll need to wake Vincent Doorface from his slumber and help him find his eyes before you can follow the clues to track down the Underground Disco's meanest judge.

Search the mansion and keep an eye out (ho ho!) for Moshlings, ghosts and monsters hidden about the place.

## WHAT'S THE DEAL?
# VINCENT DOORFACE

Vincent knows that two eyes are better than one (unless you're Zommer, of course!). This creepy looking door is friendlier than he looks, especially if you can answer his riddles!

## WHAT'S THE DEAL?
# BIG BAD BILL

Big Bad Bill is a Woolly Blue Hoodoo and knows everything about lotions, potions, hexes and spells. Never seen without their mystical Staffs of Power, Woolly Blue Hoodoos also love a party game!

## WHAT'S THE DEAL?
# GHOSTS AND GHOULS

The Haunted Mansion is full of these creepy critters! They never sleep and can get pretty bored of floating through walls all day, so are always looking for monsters to play with. They love a game of hide and seek!

# ELDER FURI'S TRAINING TIPS:
Patience is a super virtue - take your time, Moshi!

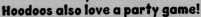

# Part 3: Saving Simon Growl

Simon Growl's all tied up and it's up to you to rescue him before he tumbles down the clock tower! There are some weird bugs around who might be persuaded to lend you a hand (or eight!) in return for some tasty treats.

## SUPER MOSHI MISSION HINT

**Pay close attention** to what **Simon** has to say - he seems to know an awful lot about what C.L.O.N.C. are up to! I've got a funny feeling your next mission might take you to Mount Sillimanjaro . . .

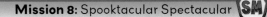

# CODE RED HELP!

ᚹᚾᛉ ᚲ⟨ᛉᚾᚲᛉᚻᛜᛜᚹ ᚹᛜ

ᛌᛁᛉ⚹ᚺᚹ ᛒᛁᚩ ᛜᛜᚪ ᛏᛜ⟨ᚴ

ᛒᛜᛎ ᛐᛁᚻ

# The Hero's Reward:

## Gabby

Gabby is a Mini Moshiphone. Whether they're flashing up funny messages, chatting to friends, playing games or composing new ringtones, they're always on hand to help Monsters. Its apps could come in pretty useful, too.

# MISSION 9:
## Snow Way Out

Simon Growl told us that C.L.O.N.C. have a base on Mount Sillimanjaro. We need to investigate – pronto! If Dr. Strangeglove really is building a Super Weapon, the Super Moshis must stop him!

## Part 1: The Cable Car

You'll need to climb right to the very top of Mount Sillimanjaro to check out what C.L.O.N.C. are doing. Unfortunately, it looks like Strangeglove has bust the cable car and it's the only way to the top! Have a poke about in the snow and see what you can dig up, you're sure to find some interesting things . . .

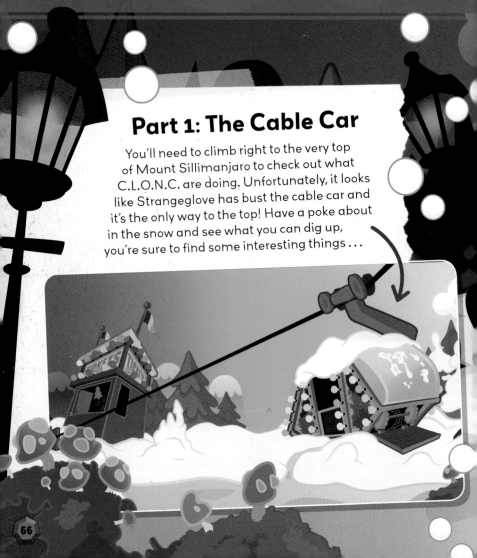

## Gabby's Apps

At least you've got Gabby to help you out, she's got loads of cool apps you can use on your mission. Although maybe not the cow one. That's just silly...

**Moshi Tunes**
– Chill out to some tunes

**Glumpass**
– for tracking down Glumps

**GooTube**
– goo to view

**Gabby's Laser**
– superpowered heat ray!

**Sicktionary** – 1001 kinds of sick explained

**Cow** – Amooosing, but not very helpful

SUPER MOSHI MISSION HINT
**Melt the snow** to make the cable car go!

# Part 2: Cabin of Super Solitude

Aha, this is my fave place in the whole Swooniverse! It's nice and quiet, it has beautiful views and it's always toasty warm. I keep all my best books here and some top equipment, too. Have a look around and help yourself to whatever you need.

Feel free to browse through the books on my shelf. Some of them will prove very useful, I'm sure! I find that when I'm reading, a fact I find in one book will make me want to pick up another. If I've written about secret stuff, I never scribble it all down in one place, so make sure you check out every shelf!

In order to get up the rest of the mountain, you'll need my specially trained super pooches, the Musky Huskies. Trouble is, they sleep like logs rather than dogs and almost nothing can wake them! You'll need to find a way to get 'em up!

Once you've woken the hounds, head to the summit and find Dr. Strangeglove!

C.L.O.N.C.

C.L.O.N.C.

WORLD DOMINATION BASE

Good Job Super Moshi!

## WHAT'S THE DEAL?
# MUSKY HUSKIES

Totally barking and slightly whiffy, Musky Huskies are the tail-chasing tearaways that will do anything for a bite to eat. They've even been spotted rummaging through trash cans searching for scraps. Maybe that's why they always look so scruffy. Take care if you decide to pet one of these greedy mucky pups — it might bite off your delicious-looking fingers. Grrrrr!

## SUPER MOSHI MISSION HINT

Wrap up warm before heading back out into the snow, but check every shelf of the cabin for useful things before you go!

# Part 3: It's a Trap!

Uh oh, Dr. Strangeglove's world domination base is a trap! This is where you'll need all your training, I'm sure. If there's one thing you should have learnt by now it's this: never trust Strangeglove!

Dial up some help from Gabby to get past the Glumps and find a way out of that cage. We have to stop C.L.O.N.C. releasing their super secret weapon!

### SUPER MOSHI MISSION HINT

Strangeglove is vain. If he's preparing for a big gig, he'll want to comb his moustache. Take any opportunity to escape while his back is turned!

## CODE RED HELP!

⊣‡ ·⌁◇< ⁝⤬ ◇◑◊ ✕◯⌿⊠✕⊟

⊣◊ ◑<◊ ⊡·⤼ ◇◑✕ ⅄⊣⊼◊◇

✳⌿◯✕⋏ ⊣⅄ ✕◯⌿⊠⊣◊✳ ‡◊⌿

▽⋏◉◇▽!

### The Hero's Reward:

# Tomba

Tomba is a Wistful Snowtot. They'll
make you feel chilly, coz they're
usually so glum. They like sad songs
but are not so keen on
Funny Bunnies.

# MISSION 10:
## Super Weapon Showdown

Elder Furi's gone missing again and C.L.O.N.C.'s Super Weapon is primed for launch! Will this be the end of Monstro City? Super Moshi, you're our only hope!

## Part 1: Around Monstro City

Our only clue is that Dr. Strangeglove's glove has been spotted running around Monstro City. Most Moshis will have fled their homes and shops in fear of C.L.O.N.C., so that may make it easier to spot the glove. It's sure to have left some kind of trail you can follow . . .

## WHAT'S THE DEAL?
## DR STRANGEGLOVE'S GLOVE!

Dr. Strangeglove got his amazing glove when his own hand was badly chewed by a Musky Husky! The glove has a mind of its own, is a deep purple colour and is *really* bad! Even without its evil owner, the glove is a slippery customer.

## Tamara Tesla's
## ~~ELDER FURI'S~~ TRAINING TIPS:

Er, well, you know I'm not very good at this, but remember that there might be things you can pick up that probably don't seem to make sense to the mission. You never know when even junk that's been dumped in Monstro City could come in useful!

## SUPER MOSHI MISSION HINT

All through the missions you've already completed, useful items will light up if you stand close to them, but the glove won't! It's always wiggling its evil fingers though, so keep an eye out for movement - high and low!

# Part 2: Into Fiery Castle

Even if you don't manage to catch the glove, you can always stay close on its tail! Of course, gloves don't have tails, but you know what I mean. If you follow the glove it might lead you to where Elder Furi is being held – or even the Super Weapon!

## WHAT'S THE DEAL?
## THE HATEKEEPER

The evil Hatekeeper is the guardian of the Fiery Castle. He's the cousin of the Super Moshi's own Gatekeeper who guards the Volcano.

The Hatekeeper really hates his cousin. He's also easily fooled. Well, he's only a stone statue, isn't he? And an evil one at that!

## Tamara Tesla's ~~ELDER FURI'S~~ TRAINING TIPS:

You can hide from nosy security cameras if you can get behind something. You can also move while they are looking elsewhere. If you're careful, you should be able to sneak past these evil surveillance machines.

## SUPER MOSHI MISSION HINT

You're gonna need all your Super Moshi training on this mission. Remember how you tricked the Glumps back in the mines? If you do find the evil lair of Strangeglove, you'll need to pretend to be an evil henchman again to get in. Just think like a super nasty C.L.O.N.C. agent and you'll be fine!

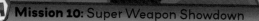

# Part 3: The Upper Levels of the Lair

In the Fiery Castle you might bump into some more of C.L.O.N.C.'s dastardly agents of doom – the rascally robots, Sprockett and Hubbs! They are a bit cleverer than the Hatekeeper, so you won't be able to trick them easily without sticking on a disguise.

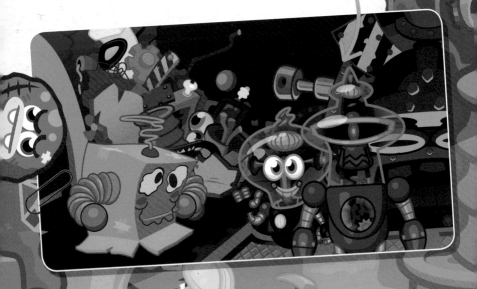

## SUPER MOSHI MISSION HINT

Even if you manage to beat Dr. Strangeglove, life in Monstro City will probably never be the same again!

See if you can put a spanner in the works to slow C.L.O.N.C. down. If we're lucky, it will give you some time to really muck up their plans. If you can stop the attack on Monstro City, you might be able to find Elder Furi.

In the end, you will have to take on Dr. Strangeglove himself. You might even find out that he isn't the worst villain in Monstro City...

## CODE RED HELP!

## The Hero's Reward:

## Wallop

Wallop is a bonkers Jolly Tubthumper. They like nothing better than hitting themselves in the face! But then, how else are they supposed to practice their drumming? They also like drumsticks and marching, but don't say "Shhhh" to them. They hate that.

To claim your exclusive virtual gift, go to the sign-in page of **MOSHIMONSTERS.COM** and enter the third word in the title on page ten. Your surprise free gift will appear in your treasure chest!

**Thank you**, Super Moshis, for your tireless hard work and **dedication** to ridding Monstro City of that dastardly Dr. Strangeglove and his wicked C.L.O.N.C. companions! The streets will be a **safer place** for Moshlings to roam now, but stay vigilant, keep your magic stones at hand, and **always be ready.** You never know when you'll be needed to fight for **peace, justice and the Moshi Way!**